A Monk's Guide to a Clean House and Mind

Shoukei Matsumoto

Translated by Ian Samhammer
Illustrated by Kikue Tamura

PENGUIN BOOKS

PENGUIN BOOKS

UK | USA | Canada | Ireland | Australia
India | New Zealand | South Africa

Penguin Books is part of the Penguin Random House group of companies
whose addresses can be found at global.penguinrandomhouse.com.

Penguin
Random House
UK

First published by Discover 21, Inc. 2011
This translation first published in Penguin Books 2018

003

Copyright © Shoukei Matsumoto, 2011, 2018
Translation copyright © Ian Samhammer, 2018
Illustrations copyright © Kikue Tamura, 2018

The moral right of the author has been asserted

Set in 10/14 pt Sabon LT Std
Typeset by Jouve (UK), Milton Keynes
Printed in Great Britain by Clays Ltd, St Ives plc

A CIP catalogue record for this book is available from the British Library

ISBN: 978-1-846-14969-6

www.greenpenguin.co.uk

Contents

Introduction

I'm a Buddhist monk at Komyoji Temple in Kamiyacho, Tokyo, Japan. I entered Komyoji Temple in 2003, becoming a monk in the Jodo Shinshu Hongwanji sect. A monk's day begins with cleaning. We sweep the temple grounds and gardens, and polish the main temple hall. We don't do this because it's dirty or messy. We do it to eliminate the gloom in our hearts.

When you visit a temple, you feel a blissful tension in the tranquil space. The gardens are well tended and spotless, without a single leaf on the ground. Inside the main temple hall, you naturally sit tall and feel alert. These things serve to calm the mind.

We sweep dust to remove our worldly desires. We scrub dirt to free ourselves of attachments. The time we spend carefully cleaning out every nook and cranny of the temple grounds is extremely fulfilling. We live simply and take time to contemplate the self, mindfully living each moment. It's not just monks who need to live this way. Everyone in today's busy world needs to do it.

Life is a daily training ground, and we are each composed of the very actions we take in life. If you live carelessly, your mind will be soiled, but if you try to live conscientiously, it will slowly become pure again. If your heart is pure, the world looks brighter. If your world is bright, you can be kinder to others.

The Zen sect of Buddhism is renowned for the cleaning practices of its monks, but cleaning is greatly valued in Japanese Buddhism in general as a way to 'cultivate the mind'. In this book, I introduce everyday cleaning methods typically employed in temples, while sharing what it's like to be a monk in training. Regarding Zen practices, I include information gleaned from discussions with Shoyo Yoshimura, a Soto Zen monk who promotes Zen vegetarian cuisine, and an *unsui* monk (Zen apprentice), Seigaku, who promotes Japanese Zen in Berlin, Germany.

I hope you enjoy applying the cleaning techniques introduced here in your home. There's nothing complicated about them. All you need is a will to sweep the dust off your heart. Your everyday domestic chores will become a way to clean your heart. This will improve the condition not just of your own mind, but of the minds of the people around you. I hope readers will discover that daily housework is an opportunity to contemplate the self.

Shoukei Matsumoto
Komyoji Temple Monk
November 2011

Understanding Cleaning

What is Cleaning?

Japanese people have always regarded cleaning as more than a common chore. It's normal here for elementary and junior high school students to clean their classroom together, although I've heard that this isn't done in schools abroad. It probably has to do with the notion in Japan that cleaning isn't just about removing dirt. It's also linked to 'cultivating the mind'.

If you visit a temple, you'll find the premises to be extremely well tended. Naturally, this is to welcome visitors, but another reason is that the act of cleaning is an important ascetic practice for the monks living and training there. Each space is cleaned, tidied and polished beautifully. While training at a temple in Kyoto, even the slightest error I made in folding or stacking clothes resulted in being given a pep talk by one of my seniors.

If you ever have the chance, observe how monks clean their temple grounds. Dressed in *samue* robes, the traditional work wear of Buddhist monks, they'll be silently engaged in their designated chores and appear cheerful and well. Cleaning isn't considered burdensome, or something you don't really want to do and wish to get over with as soon as possible. They say that one of Buddha's disciples achieved enlightenment doing nothing but sweeping while chanting, 'Clean off dust. Remove grime.' Cleaning is carried out not because there is dirt, but because it's an ascetic practice to cultivate the mind.

Rubbish

What is rubbish exactly? Things that are dirty, worn out, unusable, no longer useful, no longer needed, and so on. And yet nothing starts out as rubbish. **Things become rubbish when they are treated as rubbish.**

In Buddhism, it is believed that nothing has a physical form (*tai*). That is, there is no substance in anything in and of itself. *Mottainai*, the Japanese term for 'wasteful', originates from this word. But if something has no substance, how does it exist? Things exist because all things relate with each other to support each other's existence. Humans are the same. The people and things in your life are what makes you who you are. This is why it's not for you to judge whether something is useful, or to designate things you can't use as rubbish.

They say that the eminent monk Rennyo picked up a scrap of paper lying in the hallway one day and said, 'Even this scrap of paper is given to us by the Buddha and must not be wasted.' The Japanese idea of not being wasteful is not just about avoiding waste – it also embodies a spirit of gratitude towards objects.

People who don't respect objects don't respect people. For them, anything no longer needed is just rubbish. A child who grows up watching their parents act this way comes to perceive not just things but friends in the same way as well.

Within any object can be found the tremendous time and effort put into it – the 'heart' of the person who made it. It's important to remember to feel grateful for this when cleaning or tidying, and not handle things carelessly.

Yet we cannot store everything in a cupboard because we do not want to be wasteful. Some things, despite being a little old, still have some life left in them. Elsewhere, they would have a place to shine, but instead they are often shut away and forgotten, ending their lives without seeing the light of day. This is rather sad. Be grateful for the things that have served you and give them to people who could use them, where they can have a purpose and shine again. Appreciate the things you have right in front of you.

When to Clean and Tidy

Do you think that it doesn't matter when you clean, and that you should just do it when you find the time? I've mentioned that cleaning is a way to eliminate gloom in the mind but, even if you work really hard at sweeping and mopping, it won't really make you feel refreshed if you do it at night. In Buddhist temples there is no such thing as starting to clean after the sun has gone down.

Cleaning should be done in the morning. Do it as your very first activity of the day. The daily routine of an *unsui* monk (a Zen apprentice) starts with waking up early, washing their face and dressing, in readiness to begin cleaning and conducting services for that day.

Exposing your body to the cold in the pre-dawn air naturally makes you feel charged, filling you with energy for the tasks ahead. And cleaning quietly while the silence envelops you – before other people and plants awaken – refreshes and clears your mind. By the time everyone else is emerging, you've finished your cleaning and are all set for the day's work. Cleaning in the morning creates a breathing space for your mind so you can have a pleasant day.

At the end of the day, make sure you tidy your surroundings before going to bed. If, like an *unsui* monk, all you have to do during the day is cleaning and tidying, there'll be no need to tidy up at night. As soon as you finish using something, put it away. If you are meticulous about tidiness, there will never be anything just scattered around. This may not be easily accomplished, of course, in a regular home, which is why you should at least try to return things you have used or made a mess of to their rightful places before the day is over. It's important that your home is tidy so you can kick off the next morning feeling refreshed, as you begin your cleaning for that day. When I was training to become a monk, my roommates and I always recited evening sutras before going to bed. Doing this in a tidy room at bedtime felt refreshing and cleared the mind, leading to a deep sleep.

Cleaning and tidying are daily tasks, and what matters most is consistency. Even a short amount of time will do, so get into the habit of making a reasonable effort to clean every day. At first, it may be hard to get up early in the morning, but if you make cleaning in the morning and tidying in the evening a habit, your body and mind will feel refreshed each day.

Air Things Out

One must-do before cleaning is to open the windows to allow fresh air in. We do this at the temple to purify the air and let the crisp morning breeze in. The cool air of dawn that flows in wakes you up as it comes in contact with your skin, and you feel clean and refreshed. Filling your lungs with this fresh air naturally prepares your mind for the cleaning tasks ahead. Regardless of how much you clean things on the surface, if the air around you is stale, your mind will also feel this way.

A light breeze during the pleasant seasons of spring and autumn feels lovely. In the middle of summer, however, opening the windows allows in the stifling heat, and on winter mornings, it lets in the piercing cold air. But that's OK. **The act of cleaning is a chance to communicate with nature.**

Without the adjustments made by humans, a house would be covered in dust and its structure would weather. In a hundred years, it would fall apart and return to nature. By cleaning and looking after your home, maintaining a balance with the raw forces of nature, you can preserve it in a state that allows comfortable habitation. Humans are primarily weak creatures who cannot survive long without shelter against the elements. This is why we must make adjustments to the environment we live in.

Cleaning is a way to converse with nature. If we keep this idea in mind, then it is clear that aspects of modern life such as air-conditioning, which creates the same environment throughout summer and winter, amount to a refusal to communicate with nature. Becoming used to this will surely lead to the weakening of the body and the mind. When it's hot, it should be hot. When it's cold, it should be cold. I think that sweating as you clean, while experiencing nature, is the secret to a healthy body and mind.

Open a window and interact with nature. Become aware that you are too weak to live in the same environment as living things in the wild. Experience the gentleness and severity of nature against your skin, and feel grateful for the preciousness of the life force. Each morning, open the windows that connect you to nature and inhale the fresh air.

What to Do with Insects

Buddhists follow five precepts, and the first one requires us to abstain from taking life. All lives are interconnected and must be equally respected. You must not hurt or kill another living thing without reason. But humans have to take lives to harvest meat, fish, vegetables and so on to survive, so we must be aware of this need, and feel both remorseful and grateful.

It is important to find ways to live that will enable you to avoid killing other living things. The foundation for this is daily cleaning. Insects come out in search of food and places to lay eggs. If you leave crumbs on the dining table and dishes unwashed or don't take out the rubbish, insects will naturally emerge. Cleaning up properly after each meal is thus the first step towards abstaining from killing insects. It's important to create an environment that doesn't allow insects to breed. If you leave a bucket outside, it will collect rainwater and mosquitoes will start breeding there. Turn over buckets and other vessels that might collect water. Keep ornamental water vessels small in size and ensure cleanliness by changing the water often.

Some insects, such as termites and wasps, are dangerous if left unattended. You can prevent them from nesting by ensuring that the air is always fresh and moisture is not trapped, by pruning plants often, and improving airflow. When cutting grass, first check for leaves and excrement to ensure there are no bees or caterpillars hiding there. For the sake of both humans and insects, please be kind to and respectful of life.

Vary Your Cleaning Tasks

The various chores that monks must take care of while in training are divided among them, but these assignments change periodically. This is called *tenyaku* (role change), in which the designated location of each monk changes. For example, the person in charge of the kitchen yesterday may be in charge of the garden today. Through this system, each monk experiences every chore that must be executed at the temple.

Ascetic practice may evoke the image of someone performing a task alone and in silence, but in reality cleaning a temple requires teamwork. It's essential to know what others are doing: for example, what another person is mopping right now. You must understand the overall situation and think about the role you have to play in it, and then take certain initiatives, such as assisting others in their tasks. It is important to do things in an orderly and thorough manner while being mindful of what others around you are doing. **You must survey the overall situation before establishing what to do.** If others are working in one spot, begin at another spot.

During our training at the temple, carelessness on the part of one individual becomes the responsibility of the group as a whole. Sometimes the entire team is made to sit cross-legged on a hard wooden floor for long hours. You don't want to cause problems for others, so you really must ensure that you are doing things properly. This is an opportunity to learn that your existence is not just about yourself. This is true in everyday life, as well. It's not up to just one person to clean. Everyone must be conscious of it. Divide chores up among family members and change them around sometimes. The entire family should work as a team, conscious of each other as they perform the tasks.

We appreciate our family more when events upset our routine. For instance, a husband may first realize how dependent he is on his wife when she, who always does the cooking, is confined to bed due to illness, and he finds himself unable to make even rice porridge. Becoming aware of our shortcomings in this way is an important opportunity to try to overcome them.

Changing around household and cleaning duties is also an effective way to teach children what needs to be done. Although initiating children into this may be frustrating at first, because it would be more efficient for an adult to do the task than to help a child to do it, it is important to give children as many chores as possible. Family ties are the strongest of all human bonds. Use household chores as an opportunity to deepen them.

Be Mindful of the Weather

There are always chores that need doing at a temple, both indoors and outdoors, but we never work outside when it rains. We wait for a clear day for this. We plan our work each day while adapting to the course of nature. When we can't work outside in the temple gardens, we focus on our indoor tasks, such as polishing windows, repapering *shoji* doors, and cleaning the altar and the rooms themselves. Once the rain clears up, the ground remains damp for a short time, making it easier to pull weeds. I recommend doing outdoor work as soon as the rain has stopped.

They say that one third of an *unsui*'s day is spent cleaning, but in fact there is no end to the cleaning you can do to cultivate your mind. If you look, you will always find something to clean. On a rainy day, discard the notion that there are things to be done outside. Think flexibly and do your cleaning in tune with the movements of nature. In a regular home, it might be a good idea to establish certain arrangements, such as designating rainy days as days to do repair work. If you survey your home, you will always find things that need your attention.

Don't Put It Off Till Tomorrow

'*Zengosaidan*' is a Zen expression meaning that we must put all our efforts into each day so we have no regrets, and that we must not grieve for the past or worry about the future. In the context of cleaning to cultivate the mind, *zengosaidan* means 'Don't put it off till tomorrow'.

People today are busy, and we have all experienced going home tired, then leaving dirty dishes and laundry untended as we go to bed. But did you begin the next day feeling refreshed? Was it not depressing to wake up to the new day with yesterday's chores still to be done? It isn't just the moment you realize these things are still pending that you feel depressed. When you go to bed thinking, 'Ugh . . . I still have to do those things but I'm too tired,' you retain this gloomy feeling in your consciousness all night. Some people may even dream of working hard to finish their chores before waking up to find they have to do it all over again in real life.

Zengosaidan. This isn't just about how you feel. Do what you need to do without delay. Eliminate the seeds that distract your mind with unnecessary thoughts about things you will be dealing with tomorrow, or things that went wrong yesterday. The longer you neglect the impurities of the heart, the harder it is to remove them. Never put off what you need to do until tomorrow, and enjoy each and every day.

Useful Items

Samue Robes

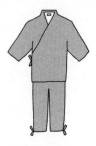

Samue robes are worn by Japanese monks when they perform their daily duties of cleaning and looking after the temple (this is called *samu)*.

Samue are easy to move in and they are perfect for cleaning, basic clerical work, and running errands around the neighbourhood. They are also useful in many other situations, and easy to wash and care for.

I prefer to wear subdued colours like deep indigo and black, but as there are a wide variety of designs available, it's not uncommon to find monks wearing patterned or brightly coloured *samue*.

Impervious to the passing of time, these simple garments are well suited for any season. Lightweight *samue* are perfect for summer, while thickly lined cotton *samue* are just right for winter.

Selecting a Samue

In summer your samue should have shorter, wider sleeves, while in winter the sleeves should have elastic at the wrists to keep warmth in. The more pockets, the better. Avoid choosing highly absorbent fashion fabrics, and instead pick a durable material that will be easy to wash.

Looking After Your Samue

Samue made out of cotton can be washed at home. If you are worried about wrinkles and creases, lightly beat the fabric with the palms of your hands, and straighten the samue back to its original shape before hanging it out to dry.

Tenugui Hand Towels

Tenugui hand towels have been in existence for so long that one could say that Japanese culture has developed along with them. In fact, along with the *samue*, a *tenugui* hand towel wrapped around the head is a perennial choice for many monks doing their chores. Some say that wrapping the towel around your head mentally prepares you for the tasks at hand.

However, it is not uncommon these days to see monks using regular terry towels in place of the Japanese *tenugui*. Apparently the Yamamotodai of the Soto Zen sect, as well as *unsui* monks of Eihei Temple, call terry-cloth towels 'work towels', and always wear them wrapped around their heads while cleaning outdoors. Since the shaved heads of monks are delicate, the *tenugui* towel provides protection against branches, doors, corners, and any other potential sources of injury. *Tenugui* towels are also useful for women who want to keep their long hair clean and protected.

I purchase nearly all of my *tenugui* towels from the specialist outlet Kamawanu, which has shops located all over the world, as well as in Japan.

Taking Care of Your Tenugui Towels

You can wash tenugui *towels as you would normally wash other items, but to prevent colours from fading, it is best to wash them by hand. After washing, hang them to dry. One of the great things about* tenugui *towels is that they dry incredibly quickly, so you can do all of your daily cleaning with just only one* tenugui.

Setta Sandals

Leather-soled *setta* sandals are the standard footwear of monks. These Japanese thongs made from natural grasses are said to have originated in the time of Senrikyuu (1522–91), one of the great masters of Japanese tea ceremony traditions.

The leather soles of *setta* sandals prevent moisture from penetrating through, even from puddles or snow, and slows down the gradual wearing down of the heel.

As *setta* sandals go well with *samue* work clothes, and are rumoured to improve the leg muscles with their thong construction, I highly recommend wearing them during your daily chores.

In recent times more and more people have been making their own cloth sandals (*nuno-zori*) for indoor wear. I would love to try making my own!

Cloth Sandals (Nuno-zori)

Nuno-zori *are made of old material that is no longer usable, sturdy string, a bamboo spatula and soles (available in shops in Japan). You'll need scissors and pliers.*

Work Gloves and Socks

Work gloves and socks are an essential for doing outdoor work. Not only do they prevent your hands and feet from getting dirtied by mud, they also protect you from thorns and glass shards. They must provide protection to your hands and feet without impeding movement.

However, for monks doing work inside the temple, bare hands and feet are the norm (though socks are permissible).

Japanese work socks (*gunsoku*) are split between the big toe and the other toes, so you can easily wear them with your *setta* sandals. It is best to select a white pair, with the heels and toes, areas most prone to get dirty, dyed grey in order to preserve a fresh and clean feeling.

Care of Work Gloves and Socks

Since dirt can be difficult to remove from work gloves if they are left unattended to, it is best to wash them with hand soap and wring them out to dry immediately after use.

Broom and Dustpan

Brooms and dustpans have been used at temples for hundreds of years. They don't require much space, nor electricity. They are lightweight and can be carried anywhere with ease, and they can be brought out without fuss when you need them. In short, they are the perfect tools for cleaning.

A small broom with shorter bristles is ideal for indoor cleaning, while a large bamboo-handled broom is better suited for sweeping up fallen leaves outdoors.

The dustpan should be light and of simple design, made out of sheet metal or a similar material. In addition to a regular dustpan, it is also useful to have a larger-sized one for outdoor work.

The Broom
Some of Buddha's disciples attained enlightenment while sweeping.

The Dustpan
One variety of dustpan made from sheet metal which has been used in Japan across the ages is called the bunka chiritori, *or 'culture dustpan'. It is lightweight and durable.*

Dust Cloth

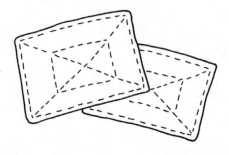

In the past, dust cloths and towels were made by folding old pieces of fabric in half and sewing them together. However, nowadays more and more people are using readymade dust cloths purchased from shops. This may perhaps be because an increasing number of households no longer own sewing machines. However, I recommend making your own dust cloths at home if you can.

Traditionally, in Zen Buddhism, practitioners wear *funzoun* clothing, that is clothes made from old pieces of fabric which are sewn together. The wearing of these repurposed rags symbolizes the importance of caring for worldly objects as well as casting out conceit. This practice removes impurities from the heart.

As with *funzoun* clothing, the dust cloth contains the heart of those who carefully put their time and energy into making it.

The Dust Cloth

In the world of Buddhism re-using items is a standard which guides our day-to-day lives. There is no such thing as making a dust cloth out of a brand new piece of fabric. Instead, we find a piece of fabric that can no longer fulfil its original purpose, and make it into a new dust cloth. This commitment to treasure objects until they can no longer be used or repurposed is at the heart of Buddhism.

Bucket

When it comes to cleaning, water, a gift from the heavens, is the ultimate natural cleaning tool. As we must in some way contain this gift, the bucket is another tool that we must treasure.

When cleaning out of doors, utilize rainwater; when cleaning indoors, use leftover bath water. It is of utmost importance that we do not waste this invaluable resource.

Placing a bucket directly on the wooden floor can leave a ring of water behind. To prevent this from happening, place the bucket on top of a dust cloth. When removing the dust cloth from the floor, be especially careful so as not to spill any water.

The Bucket

Many people will have used some kind of bucket at some point during their childhood. The ideal bucket for cleaning should be light to carry but sturdy: a metal bucket is best. However, as metal objects have a tendency to rust, make sure that you remove any moisture from the bucket when you have finished using it.

Brush and Feather Duster

A brush is ideal for cleaning lacquer ware, *shoji* screens, and other delicate objects that can be easily damaged.

As dust tends to collect in the frames of a *shoji* screen, trying to clean such small areas with a dust cloth would be ineffective. The screen is made out of paper, so you cannot clean it with water either, as this would simply spread the dust around and makes it look even dirtier than before. With that in mind, a brush is the perfect tool to tackle these challenges. If you brush the screen carefully enough, there's no need for a dust cloth at all.

When it comes to cleaning the family altar, including the bodhisattva figure and the ancestors' name tablets, a soft feather duster is ideal. After briefly joining your hands together and paying your respects, remove dust from top to bottom in a gentle stroking motion. As long as you use a feather duster manufactured in Japan, even delicate figures decorated with gold leaf will be safe from damage.

The Feather Duster

Feather dusters produced in Japan are made by talented craftsmen who carry on the tradition of manufacturing quality tools by hand. Keeping in mind the care put into these objects by their makers, we as users can also put our own hearts into the cleaning we do.

Feather dusters with long handles are especially useful for thoroughly removing dust from the ceiling, starting from one side of the room and going towards the other.

Sickle, Pruning Shears and Grindstone

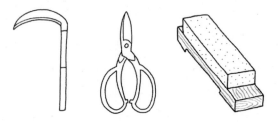

When caring for your garden, a sickle and pruning shears are vital tools. After you have used them, it is essential to give each the maintenance it needs. In order to do this, you will need a grindstone. If you simply leave them as they are they will rust. To prevent rusting, thoroughly wash and remove any leftover soil and moisture. You should sharpen the sickle with the grindstone so that it's ready for immediate use.

Using a sickle or shears that have not been sharpened properly requires much more effort and will lead to exhaustion or even injury. It's best to have garden tools at hand that one can use effortlessly at any time.

The Sickle
Not too big, not too small. The best sickle is one which is large but not difficult to wield. Sickles should be held with the thumb, index and middle fingers, with the ring and pinky fingers lightly wrapped around the handle.

The Pruning Shears
Take care of your pruning shears as if they were one of your own children. Before using them, I look at the plant from top to bottom, then I find areas that need pruning and carefully remove that part of the plant with my shears.

The Grindstone
I use a grindstone for sharpening my sickle and shears. If your grindstone is in poor condition then your blades will also become of poor quality. Rinse your grindstone off with water after use, remove any moisture, and wrap it in a tenugui or other cloth before storing.

1

The Kitchen, Bathroom and Toilet

応量器

The Kitchen

The cook position at a Zen temple, the *tenzo*, is extremely important. This role is permitted only to those who are deeply committed to their search for enlightenment.

Tenzo epitomize those on the path to enlightenment who possess pure hearts, unplagued by worldly desire, so it is essential that they devote their hearts and souls to work in the kitchen.

At an ordinary temple, the kitchen is normally used to prepare food for parishioners and town council members who come to visit, so it is much bigger than a kitchen you might find in an average household. The sink, the pots and even the sieves are incredibly large.

When I was a child, I always looked forward to the local women's association New Year's gathering at the local temple, where they would make delectable hot-pot meals.

Since so many people can cook together in these large temple kitchens, they are always polished to perfection, with all the cooking instruments returned to their proper places.

If a kitchen is kept in good order, anybody who needs to work there can immediately begin to do so with comfort and ease, keeping preparation times short and allowing delicious dishes to be served while they are still hot.

One thing that I would like you to pay particular attention to while cooking is to shut any drawer or cabinet door you have opened. When you're busy it is easy to forget to do it, but **this is a sign of your heart being untidy.**

After taking something out, you must close what you have opened. This not only helps to prevent dust from coming in contact with tableware, but also keeps your heart tidy and clean.

The cornerstone of a monk's diet is vegetarian food. Meat and fish are, of course, prohibited, but vegetables that have a strong odour such as onions, leeks and garlic, are also not acceptable for cooking.

Ingredients like *konbu* (a variety of kelp) and shiitake mushrooms are popular with many of the monks I am acquainted with for the exquisite *dashi* soup stock that they can produce. Once you become used to a diet based on mild vegetables, the ability to identify even the most subtle of flavours with your tongue enhances the joy of eating, greatly improving your sense of taste.

Dishes that feature seasonal ingredients and highlight their natural flavours are also key in a monk's diet. As a result, unusual cooking spices and large amounts of cooking oil are rarely required; instead we use ingredients in the most natural way possible. Since only a small number of kitchen appliances and implements are involved in the preparation of a meal, cleaning up is always very easy.

It is essential to leave as little cooking waste as possible. Using up all or as much of your ingredients as possible will naturally reduce the amount of waste you produce. For example, if you are cooking Japanese radish (mooli), you can also use both the leaves and the skin, which can be turned into *kinpira* (a side dish containing julienned carrots and other root vegetables cooked in soy sauce and sugar). If there are still leftovers, they should be used as fertilizer whenever feasible.

Even if you are part of a regular household, you will find that making an effort to consume a diet as similar to a monk's as possible brings many benefits. Cleaning up after meals becomes much easier, and the more you stick with this diet the more you will appreciate it.

The *tenzo* takes a meal's ingredients into his heart, and it is said that through the preparation of vegetarian meals, he becomes at one with the food he cooks. You can prepare hearty healthy meals with fresh, seasonal ingredients and clean, neat tools.

Let's do our best to create a clean and comfortable kitchen to work in.

How to Clean the Sink

Baking soda is particularly effective for cleaning sinks. To prevent water stains from forming around the sink and drain, be sure to completely dry any leftover water after using it. You should also always empty out any food left over in the drain catcher. Do not leave this to be done the next day.

How to Clean Cooking Utensils

Soaking cooking utensils that have been burned or dirtied in the sink and leaving them until the next day is not acceptable. Wash immediately after use: this is the way of Zen monks. Dishes and other items that are more difficult to clean should first be rinsed with water (hot water is best) so as to loosen any stuck-on food, and then, using a metal scouring pad, scrubbed until clean. Baking soda is also effective when tackling pots and pans. Don't forget to dry everything off when you are done.

The Secret to Washing Dishes

The most important thing about washing dishes is not to allow them to pile up. In order to do this:

1. *Visualize what kind of meal you are going to cook and do only the work necessary for this meal.*

2. *Use any free time during the cooking process to wash dirtied dishes and tidy up the kitchen.*

If you are able to do these two things, the cooking process itself will become shorter, drastically reducing the amount of water you use for washing dishes, and also the amount of time you spend clearing up after a meal. Cleaning up after cooking will become a breeze.

The Bathroom

What comes to your mind when picturing a bathroom? Taking a nice soak in the bath after washing all of the day's dirt away with the shower? Somewhere to relax after a hard day and refresh the spirit? I think that many people probably have this image in their mind.

According to tradition, *unsui* monks of the Soto Zen sect must obey the 'Three Mandas of Silence', which forbid them to speak in three areas of the temple: the *zodo* hall (where monks meditate, eat and sleep), the *yokusu* (bathroom), and the *tousu* (toilet).

The one element that connects the Three Mandas of Silence is water. Water, the basis of all life, enters and circulates through our body before leaving it and becoming part of nature again in these three areas, and silence enables us to be mindful of the cycle of life. It is therefore very important to keep the hall, bathroom and toilet meticulously clean.

The way in which a Japanese monk takes a bath is predetermined, with those just beginning on their path to enlightenment being accompanied by their elders to be instructed in it. Because of this, even when taking a bath you are always extremely aware of yourself. Before entering the bath itself you must wash your body thoroughly, making sure to remove all dirt. You do this in *seiza*, a posture in which the legs are bent at the knees and folded beneath one's body. In order to save water monks collect it in a pail.

At the temple, although there are baths large enough to accommodate up to ten people at once, the ideal is that **even if 100 people were to enter the bath at the same time the water should remain clear like that of a river.** The idea is to make as little noise as possible when entering the bath. Splashing around loudly when bathing breaks the silence and contributes to the waste of water.

The only object that a monk uses in the bath at a temple is a pail. Monks bring their own soap and *tenugui* towel (though other kinds of towels are permissible). Before going to the bathroom, a monk makes sure that all his bathing items are in order. Then he puts the pail back in its proper place in the bathroom after use, and checks that the taps are turned to face the same direction. Everything must feel as though it is in the perfect place.

As this is an area closely related to water, the basis of all life, it is natural for one's instincts to reveal themselves. Simply put, the bathroom, like the toilet, is a place in which others cannot see you. Because of this, the strong ego can be revealed in this room.

Due its nature, we always make sure that the bathroom

is scrubbed clean in a thorough and methodical manner. Areas that are particularly prone to dirt if cleaning is put off should be cleaned in a scrupulous manner. This will, in turn, keep the heart pure.

If you enter a damp bathroom, your heart also becomes damp. If mould grows in a bathroom, then mould also grows in your heart. If the body is washed sloppily, then impurities of the heart cannot be removed.

If you allow dirt left by the basis of life, water, to form, then impurities will accumulate within your heart as well. Conversely, **if the bathroom is kept clean, then you can keep your heart clean as well.**

'The highest excellence is like water.' These words from the Tao Te Ching convey that the ideal way of life is like water: flexible and calm.

To remove impurities from your heart, be sure to keep the bathroom sparkling clean.

How to Clean the Bathroom

First, scrub the floor clean so that you can sit comfortably, even in a seiza position. Use a Japanese tawashi or a similar scrub brush to remove any mineral deposits (however, surfaces that can be damaged easily should be cleaned with a sponge rather than a tawashi). Use baking soda on grime that is more difficult to remove.

After cleaning the bathroom, you may find yourself so relaxed that you hum without thinking. However, as the bathroom is one of the Three Mandas, why not try from time to time cleaning it in complete silence instead?

The Toilet

This is where the true colours of a household are revealed. However, while many people pay particular attention to cleaning the entrance of their home before guests arrive, not all give the same amount of attention to the toilet (*tousu*).

When guests use your toilet, they are entering a private room alone. Since, as with the bathroom, this is a place where one can let one's guard down, it is likely that they will notice even the minutest of details: a dirtied toilet, dust on the floor, an empty toilet paper roll.

If the toilet is a poorly kept room where guests are unable to relax, this will impact negatively on their impression of both your home and the head of the household: they will not feel truly welcome.

The toilet is one of the areas that Zen monks always put a great deal of effort into keeping clean.

Adherents of Zen Buddhism also believe that Ucchusma (also known as Ususami Myou in Japanese) attained enlightenment in the toilet, thus making it a holy space.

Since the toilet is an area that allows us to expel impurities, it is vital that our cleaning of it be thorough, leaving not even a fingerprint behind. Incidentally, as one of the pious acts Ucchusma performs is to 'cleanse all impurities of the world', we place divine statues of Ucchusma in the toilet.

The toilet etiquette carefully observed by Zen monks, established by Master Dogen (AD 1200–1253), is to **utter not a single word, and to keep the area clean.**

Even at the temples of Pure Land Buddhism, where there are separate toilets normally reserved for visitors, I have never come across a toilet that was dirty or not kept in good order. Regardless of which temple you go to, the toilets will be clean. Someone is always at the ready to keep them this way, making sure that toilet slippers are properly placed for their guests (in Japan, house slippers are taken off before entering the toilet, and we change into a second pair of slippers used only in the toilet).

Those who use a well-maintained toilet can sense its cleanliness on their skin, and are able to relax during their time there. In addition, a well-maintained toilet naturally creates an environment that encourages the user to use it in a tidy manner so that the next person can also enjoy the same level of cleanliness.

Monks on the path to enlightenment at Eihei Temple don't wear slippers in the toilet at all. Although they wear special slippers while inside the *zodo* hall, they remove them at the *tousu* and enter barefoot.

According to one of my monk friends, the *tousu* there is so clean that one could lie down on its floor, and when entering, one is as solemn as if taking part in a ceremony.

Since the toilet should be a place that is both calm enough for you to be able to relax, and clean enough to make you conscious of the way in which you use it, always endeavour to clean this room as often as possible.

Toilet Etiquette

Although it is standard practice for all temples to keep their toilets clean, Zen temples are particularly meticulous when it comes to cleaning their toilets.

Regardless of how many toilets there are, cleaning should, at the very least, be done in the morning and at night. The tousu used by unsui monks is kept particularly clean: after wiping down the wooden floor and toilet itself with an old dust cloth, any leftover hairs, dust or paper are removed as well. The ends of the toilet paper are folded into a triangle.

*The basic secret to keeping a toilet clean is to **use it in a clean way**. If everyone makes an effort to use the toilet in a clean way, **when it's your turn to use it, you'll find yourself leaving the toilet cleaner than when you first found it, in turn helping to preserve the next user's awareness of its cleanliness**.*

The principle of cleaning your own toilet is very much like the idea that even just one or two lines of graffiti in a public toilet can immediately cause it to become filthier and filthier.

Since the toilet is clean, you do not leave it dirty. Since you have not left it dirty, the toilet will stay clean. When this rule is broken, the toilet becomes dirty immediately. The first step to keeping your toilet clean is to adopt this mantra into your own life.

2

Other Parts of the Home

Floors

When it comes to cleaning a temple, polishing the floor is as basic a chore as it gets. **For many monks, a day does not go by that they don't clean the floors of the temple corridors.**

Since the floors are thoroughly polished day in and day out, every inch of them is beautiful, with their surface, blackened through hundreds of years of use, taking on an almost translucent, fossilized look. You can walk through a carefully maintained temple all day long in white socks without worrying about discolouring them. There is no dust or grime to speak of.

It is the job of the monks to perform the upkeep on these beautifully preserved floors. They are polished every day whether they appear to need it or not.

When you are polishing the floor, you are polishing your heart and your mind.

The point of housework is to clean up dirt and grime, isn't it? So you might be wondering what is the point of cleaning something that is already spotless. But for monks the physical act of polishing the floor is analogous to cleaning the earthly dirt from your soul. This grime accumulates in your body and poisons your mind. This manifests itself as a dirty room and cluttered surroundings. Wipe your floor and see. Each blemish you find is a sign of unrest in your mind. Once you learn how to see how your inner turmoil manifests itself through your surroundings, you can reverse engineer this, mastering yourself by mastering the space in which you live.

It goes without saying that dust will accumulate in a home that is never cleaned. Just as you have finished raking the leaves, more are sure to fall. It is the same with your mind. Right when you think you have cleaned out all the cobwebs, more begin to form. Adherence to the past and misgivings about the future will fill your head, wresting your mind from the present. This is why we monks pour ourselves heart and soul into the polishing of floors. Cleaning is training for staying in the now. Therein lies the reason for being particular about cleanliness.

Kyoto's Jissoin Temple is known for the way its floor reflects the beautiful autumn leaves from the trees that surround it. But just how much polishing does it take to achieve such a beautiful, reflective black lustre? Why not polish the floor in your home as if you were polishing a mirror that will reflect your soul?

How to Polish the Floor

Before we polish the floor in a temple, we must sweep it thoroughly. Only once the sweeping is complete can we begin wiping. Dip a cloth in a bucket of water, wring it with all your might, then glide it across the surface of the floor. We don't use any soap, and there is no need to dry the floor. Your carefully wrung out cloth should contain a minimum of moisture, meaning that the floor dries out shortly after the cleaning rag passes over it.

As you do this, avoid any unnecessary thoughts, instead allowing your body to focus only on the task in hand. When doing this alone, you should be looking inward. When doing this with others, allow yourself to notice those around you, being conscious of your role in the team effort.

Guest Rooms

The *tokonoma* (a decorative alcove in a Japanese-style room) became a fixture in every Japanese home during the Edo period (1615–1867), and has come to be a treasured symbol of Japanese culture. The *tokonoma* usually contains a *kakejiku* (hanging scroll) on the wall of the alcove, with flowers and incense on the floor beneath it. It may also contain a simply decorated shelf. The *tokonoma* is the face of your guest room, and should be carefully considered when you are expecting company.

Even in hard-to-see places such as the tracks of *shoji* doors, you must not cut corners. Though it may be difficult to see, leftover grime and clutter will negatively affect the climate of the room. Clutter that is hastily stowed away in drawers before the guest shows up will give an air of disorder to the room. Be sure to clean even places that are well out of your reach.

Once you have cleaned the room in its entirety, survey it carefully. Is there any dirt or dust? Are there any unnecessary items out? Is everything orderly and organized? Since a guest is coming, also make sure that you are stocked up with drinks, snacks, clean linen, etc. This should never be overlooked! Everything needs to be done to make sure that your guest has the most comfortable stay possible.

At the temple we believe that if guests are visiting on business, it should be our goal to create a space free of distractions where they can talk and work. That is the key to good hospitality. If the surroundings are dirty or the windows have fingerprints on them, this will tug at the mind of your guests, making it difficult for them to say what they want to say. Overly gaudy decorations should be avoided as well for the same reason. What you want instead is simple beauty, and decorations that will make your guests feel a lightness or perhaps even a playfulness in the room. The ultimate goal is to put each of your guests' minds at ease.

How to Clean the Tokonoma

Clean once with a dry towel, then with a wet one. If you commit your mind fully to the task, you can bring out the brilliance of the area with a dry rag alone. Once it is clean, hang a seasonal kakejiku and put out a simple arrangement of flowers.

The *Butsuma*

Monks often visit people's homes in order to recite a sutra for a recently departed loved one. When we arrive, the owner will meet us at the front door and lead us to the *butsuma* (Buddhist altar). The location of the *butsuma* depends on the family. Some people have it near the entrance while some have it in the living room. Although homes come in all shapes and sizes, there is one common thread that I see over and over again: **families that do not take good care of their *butsuma*.** In extreme cases I have even seen the space around the altar turned into a veritable storage space for dusty, unused furniture and exercise equipment. I cannot help but feel bad when I behold such a sight.

Do you have, or have you seen, a *butsuma*? A *butsuma* is a place where the spirit of Buddha rests. Many people think that the altar is simply a place to pay respect to deceased family members. Actually, the altar enshrines the souls of those who have passed on and become a part of Buddha themselves. In other words, **your altar is your**

family's own little temple. It is a place where you can express gratitude, and where Buddha will come to you to ease your heart and soul. Even in a small apartment, surely you can get creative and dedicate one small shelf to your own altar.

Once a day, whether morning or evening, bring a small offering of food to the altar, then put your hands together in quiet prayer. This will soothe your heart and allow you a little more peace of mind throughout your daily routine.

You should think of the space around your altar as temple grounds. You would never litter or clutter up the sacred area around a temple or a church, and so you should treat your *butsuma* the same way. Commit yourself to keeping this space as clean and tidy as possible.

How to Clean Your Butsuma

Just as you would with your guest room, keep the cleaning of your butsuma simple and gentle. Your goal should be to provide a quiet, relaxing atmosphere for all that enter. You may want to bear in mind the following:

1 *Keep the ashes in your incense holder flat and clean. If your incense holder is becoming full of incense cinders, use a strainer to collect them. Once you have tidied up, the incense should be able to burn entirely without going out.*

2 *Never touch the golden parts of your altar with a rag or your hand. Instead, use a feather duster to gently remove the dust.*

3 *Take great care when cleaning all the other parts of your altar. Use a soft cloth to dust the metal parts. You can rub the colour off if you use a coarse cloth or detergent, so do this at your own risk. I personally use a cloth that is specially designed to clean the various metal tools and decorations in a Buddhist altar. If your altar should ever require any kind of serious repair or maintenance, do seek the help of a professional.*

Shoji doors

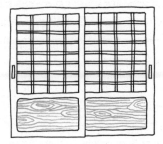

Repairing *shoji* (paper doors or screens) is one of a monk's tasks. Sometimes visitors to the temple, especially young children, will inadvertently poke a hole in the delicate *shoji*. It is our job to repaper the affected area as soon as possible. But even with no one poking holes in them, *shoji* can become dirty and weathered over time. Since they are made of paper, we cannot simply clean them with a rag. Even if there is no damage, the paper has to be replaced at regular intervals, namely each time the seasons change.

Nowadays products are designed for easy use and easy disposal. In such a world, we cannot really expect that people will have a deep appreciation for the things they consume. However, *shoji* are something that you do not simply replace every time they break, and there is no such thing as *shoji* paper that will never tear. In comparison to most modern conveniences, *shoji* are a pretty burdensome thing to own. If you do not put a little bit of elbow grease into them regularly, they are nearly impossible to maintain. **But this inconvenience can teach us a lot in our modern world.** By using and maintaining such a device, we can gain a better understanding of all that goes into the various gadgets around us. By replacing the paper in your *shoji* by yourself, you will foster a deeper appreciation for your surroundings. Not only that, but the effort you put in will lend a warmth to the air that your guests will be able to sense in every corner of every room.

I recommend having your children help you. They are much less likely to poke a hole in the paper that they helped install.

How to Repaper Your Shoji

Back in the day there were different sizes of shoji paper based on the size of your frame. Today, however, many people use a one-size-fits-all approach.

1 Use a moist sponge to dissolve the glue on the paper. Once you have done so, carefully peel the paper away from the frame.

2 Wipe the frame clean and then allow it to dry completely.

3 Use a piece of tape to fasten one corner of the new paper to the frame. This will be your starting point. Using a special shoji paintbrush and paste, thoroughly coat the contact points on the frame. Being careful to act while the paste is still wet, roll the paper on to the frame.

4 Cut off the extra paper, trimming it to the size of your frame.

Lighting

It is not easy to clean light fixtures in high places every day. Even at the temple we do not do this daily. But my recommendation for hard-to-reach spots is to set up a cleaning schedule. Setting a regular schedule for cleaning such places is a good way to keep them looking great, and to avoid overlooking them. The monks at the Eihei Temple take care of these spots when the date ends in a '3' or an '8', in other words the 3rd, the 8th, the 13th, etc., of the month. These areas can require many hands, so try to enlist family members or friends.

Back before the light bulb, light was only available until the sun went down. Even in today's age of electric light, we should do our best to keep sources of illumination free of grime or anything else that might obscure them. In the world of Buddhism, light is a symbol of wisdom and compassion. My temple is called Komyoji or Bright Light Temple.

The ultimate goal of Buddhist teachings is to conquer the suffering in people's lives and open them up to enlightenment. In most cases we regard the root of human suffering as *mumyo*. Literally translating as 'no light', *mumyo* refers to the condition of being figuratively lost in the dark. Since you are unable to see the true nature of what is around you, your mind succumbs to worry and anxiety.

Wisdom is your most powerful weapon against *mumyo*. Wisdom allows us to know the world around us as it truly is. The light that appears to be shining from behind the head of some statues of Buddha is an expression of His sincere wish to rescue the people of the world from this darkness. By allowing the light of Buddha's wisdom to shine upon them, people can escape their earthly doubts and misgivings.

Keeping sources of light in your home clear and free of grime will allow the light of wisdom to pour in, vanquishing your *mumyo* and easing your troubled mind.

How to Clean Your Lights

First, remove the dust with a feather duster. Then, wring out a moist cloth and wipe the surfaces carefully. Do this with a friend or loved one if possible. One person can support the stepladder while the other person works atop it. The person at the bottom can also hand tools and supplies to their partner as needed. Clean the lamps and fixtures gently, as if you are polishing your heart and soul to make them shine their brightest.

3

Personal Items

Clothes

I heard recently that more and more people don't change into a different set of clothes with each new season. It seems that this is due in part to the popularity of garments that can be worn all year round, and in part to the availability of inexpensive clothing at the beginning of every new season. Of course, I realize that reducing the burden of having to change into a new set of seasonal clothes has practical benefits. However, just like spring cleaning, changing what you wear when a new season comes is beneficial in another, deeper way.

When you mark the changing of the seasons with a change in your clothes you can also **refresh your heart.**

If you don't reflect the seasons in this way, you miss out on an important opportunity to refresh your heart, and put yourself at risk of having a lacklustre year.

To show your appreciation for the clothes which have, up until then, taken care of you, be sure to wash them or send them out to be cleaned. You must not think 'I'll just wash the clothes when I wear them next year', and leave them dirty. To ensure that you can comfortably wear your clothes the following year, be sure to follow the Zen concept of 'not putting it off till tomorrow'.

At the Pure Land Buddhism Temple of Hongan, monks change into a different set of clothes twice a year on the 1st of June and the 1st of October. When changing into her new season's clothes, the grandmother of Komyou Temple (actually the chief priest's mother) always says, 'Looks like I get to do this again this year' in a graceful tone, reflecting both on the flow of time and on the turn of the season.

It is important to express gratitude at the changing of the seasons. **Only those who do this truly know how to achieve closure in their feelings.**

Before changing into the new season's garments, those from the ending season must be washed. Sweat and dirt that have not been removed can cause odour to develop and stains to form. Since clothes in storage are also prone to being eaten by insects, make sure to thoroughly clean and dry them in the open air before putting them away.

This is also the time to get clothes mended. Since monks wear their robes for a very long time, the thread around the sleeves often becomes loose, while the collar and hemlines tend to slacken. Before we put our robes away we make sure such issues have been addressed.

Laundry

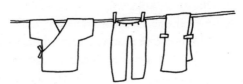

In this day and age, doing the laundry without a washing machine has become unfathomable. It isn't so long ago, however, that clothes were washed using a washboard, soap and lye.

Though most *unsui* monks now use a communal washing machine, hard-to-remove dirt and items that cannot be washed in the washing machine, such as *setta* sandals, are washed by hand.

If there is a stain on your clothes, that spot becomes the focal point of your attention, making you unable to relax for the entire day.

If you do not feel that way about stains on your clothes, this is proof of indifference about the way you present yourself. It is a sign that your heart is confused.

Wearing a pure white shirt allows you to draw in your feelings. Removing stains and black spots helps to keep the heart lively and fresh.

With this in mind, the colour of the underwear worn by monks is white.

Underneath our black outer robes, we wear a white robe and a white inner robe. Both the robe and inner robe must be white. When you become a monk, the white colour of your underwear as well as its cut are predetermined.

Though one of the reasons for choosing white is that it provides a feeling of cleanliness, the primary reason for choosing white is to rid oneself of unnecessary ornamentation. The shaving of our heads, the garments we wear and the things we carry, even the way we perform certain tasks, are all designed as to expel vanity and allow us to remain simple and modest while following the teachings of Buddha.

Putting on white underwear makes me feels as though a fresh wind is blowing over my body. Wearing white clothes over your white underwear seems to communicate to your body a feeling of cleanliness. I highly recommend to those who rarely wear white underwear to try it least once.

Speaking about laundry, when it comes to drying clothes, people now increasingly rely on tumble dryers. And among those who dry their clothes outside, there are many who wear their clothes straight from the washing line without having folded them up and put them away first.

Of course, doing things this way saves time, but cutting corners on one task leads us to cut corners on another and then another, leading to a weakening of the heart.

Use energy from the sun and dry your clothes in a natural setting. Changing your clothes also begins with putting things back where they belong, and then taking them out when they are needed.

Laundry needs to be done every day. **Wash. Dry. Fold. Put away.**

While doing this requires time and energy, one way to make laundry tasks less onerous is to reduce the amount of clothes you have to wash. However, it is vital that you complete your daily tasks on the day they should be done.

If you put this philosophy into everyday practice, you will soon find a new rhythm to your life, something which will help more than anything else to wipe away impurities. However, if you neglect your duties, you'll find that your feelings, just like the laundry, have remained unwashed, allowing dirt to accumulate in your heart.

The things you must wash and rinse in your daily life are not limited to clothing. With just the smallest bit of neglect, the heart too can become neglected and begin to fill with worldly desires. This is why we must do the laundry.

How to Do the Laundry

Fabrics made out of cotton can wrinkle easily when wet, so after washing them, immediately pat the wrinkles and hang up to dry. I know that sometimes people think that it's OK to just let the clothes dry without bothering to do this. However, **your task won't be complete once you have washed the clothes**.

For monks, the most common types of stains are ink stains, tea stains and soup stains. Ink and tea stains are usually found in smaller areas of clothing because we have not paid enough attention to what we were doing. To remove a stain, lightly dampen the spot, and then wash it with soap. Once you have rinsed it with water, the stain usually disappears, but in cases when it won't budge, use baking soda or natural bleaching solutions to remove it. This also works well for perspiration stains or for whites which have lost their brightness. Vinegar makes a wonderful fabric softener.

At temples, we do not dry our laundry where it can be seen from the outside. To avoid embarrassment when guests and parishioners visit, we use an area at the back where the wind blows well.

Do not put off laundry for another day. Even if it is just a small amount, be sure to do a wash every day and dry it immediately. If you do this, you will look neat and no longer require a large amount of clothes.

Ironing

The kinds of clothes that I want to wear in my daily life are clothes that are not wrinkled. Even the white robes that we wear underneath our black outer robes are neatly ironed and pressed. By doing this, **our hearts remain crisp and fresh for the whole day.**

Though wrinkles are normally viewed as a sign of age, there are many active monks in their 80s and 90s who not only have young hearts, but look young as well, with few wrinkles to be seen. This can be none other than a sign of **the unity of body and mind: the body reflects the heart, and the heart reflects the body.**

Always iron your clothes to keep your heart fresh and young. And of course, make sure to fold any clothes you have ironed carefully so as not to wrinkle them again.

How to Iron

When ironing, visualize yourself ironing out the wrinkles in your heart. This is a special way that Zen monks do their ironing.

Spilled wax from a candle can be removed by placing a piece of newspaper over the wax, and then placing the iron on top. Mysteriously, the wax comes off perfectly.

Wax which has been spilled on clothes can be removed in a similar manner. (Please be careful when doing this!)

Storage

Now that we have taken care of washing, drying and folding the clothes, it is time to store them. But first, insect repellent needs to be prepared. The insect repellent we use in temples is either the unscented kind, or incense purchased at a traditional incense shop, perfumed with naturally extracted camphor or else Japanese cypress tree essential oil. (When monks change into their new season's clothes at Komyou Temple, insect repellent is purchased from a long-established incense shop in Kyoto.)

The best kind of wood for your wardrobe is **paulownia wood.**

The Best Storage

Paulownia is so good at keeping insects at bay that some temples with paulownia chests go without any insect repellant at all. Of course, wardrobes made out of paulownia wood are not inexpensive so you may hesitate before purchasing one. However, high-quality furniture does last a long time, so if you're thinking of handing such a piece of furniture down as an heirloom, paulownia wood is worth considering.

Tableware

The tableware used at temples is extremely basic. Monks normally use the same sets of simply adorned tableware over the course of many decades: this consists of earthenware teacups and painted lacquer bowls.

Even if they are a little expensive, we choose classic pieces that can be used day in and day out. Purchasing such items ensures not only that they will last a long time, but also that if one piece should happen to break you will be able to replace it. This makes it possible to purchase only what you need.

Without food we cannot remain alive. . The dishes that you eat out of are not merely dishes, but also **important vessels that help to support life. They are tools to preserve life, so be sure to take the utmost care of them.**

Zen monks use *oryoki* nesting tableware sets, and in Zen monasteries, meals are taken following strict rules. Pure Land Buddhists do not use such sets, but they are made in such a logical way that practitioners are said to find them deeply interesting.

Oryoki sets consist of six bowls, chopsticks, a spoon and some other items, all of which are wrapped in a *fukusa* (silk cloth).When it's time to eat, the bowls are removed from the *fukusa*, lined up on the table, and then we silently wait to receive our meal. At breakfast, lunch and dinner, we use three of the six bowls. However, depending upon the time of day the size of bowl differs.

The largest bowl, in which all the others are nestled, is called the *zuhatsu*, and it is supposed to represent the head of Buddha. Because of this, we cannot place it directly on the table, so instead we rest it on top of the smallest bowl.

When the priests serving the meal stop in front of me, I join my hands in prayer after extending out my bowl, and then receive rice, soup and pickles or another side dish. Since the *zodo* hall is one of the Three Mandas, we eat without uttering a word, keeping our hearts silent.

Unsui monks do not wash their dishes. This is because these are washed naturally during the course of the meal. Monks have a piece of lacquer ware (*hassetsu*) that comes with a special spatula with 2.5 centimetres of cloth sewn on to the handle. They use the spatula to scrape any leftover food from the largest bowl to the smallest bowl when receiving their tea at the end of the meal. After that, **hot water is poured into the bowls for purification. Once the monks have drunk this water, the bowls are clean.** They are then dried with a cloth.

In Zen monasteries, to drop a bowl on the ground is such a great sin that the person responsible must go to

the residences of all the elder monks to apologize. Dropping a bowl shows that you are not taking care of it. Dishes must be carefully held in both hands. Holding things in this way displays a sense of natural sophistication and shows that you take care of each and every thing you hold. I recommend that you give it a try.

'A single drop of water left in the ladle can be drawn by a hundred million people' goes one of our sayings. Just one drop of water can provide us with an opportunity to expand our consciousness of the bigger picture.

The emphasis on conservation which is at the heart of our way of life is not just an effort to be green. **In order to remove impurities from the heart, you must reduce wastefulness in your heart.**

Even though we use regular dishes when entertaining guests, we still do our utmost to reduce waste. We use small amounts of dishwashing liquid to clean the dishes, and baking soda on our cutting boards and other cooking tools as a bleaching agent. Most importantly, we utilize natural cleaning methods that are kind to both the environment and the body.

Dishes are one of the tools that support life. Please take great care when using them.

Oryoki

In practice, all of our daily meals are eaten out of the six oryoki bowls. Since all the bowls differ slightly in size, they can be nested within one another, making the set extremely compact.

Oryoki sets contain a napkin, a cleaning cloth, a hattan (*a place mat to be used under the largest bowl*), a small spatula, a spoon, chopsticks, a mizuita (*a water board, whose origin and purpose are currently unknown but which is still included in* oryoki sets), *and a silk wrapper.*

応量器

4

Repairs and Maintenance

Repairs

When using any sort of item over time, it is impossible to prevent it from developing signs of wear and tear. However, since most items usually wear down in specific areas, repairing them will allow you to continue using them for some time.

One of the principles of a Buddhist lifestyle is to take care of things and **repair** them.

The *unsui* monks of Eihei Temple **designate days that contain the numbers '4' and '9' for mending clothes** that have become raggedy and old. This is called *shikunichi*, literally meaning four and nine days. Even ordinary households should try designating *shikunichi* days as a time for mending items and performing maintenance around the home.

Nowadays it is very easy to find a wide variety of items that are exactly alike and more or less serve the same function. When something breaks, rather than repairing it, many people buy a replacement because this is faster and cheaper. However, if you continue to live your life in this way, your relationships with others will begin to resemble how you relate to objects. This will only lead to the exhaustion of your heart.

If you use an object for as long as you can carefully, repairing it when necessary, you will find that not only your relationship with objects begins to change, but so will the way you relate to people. This will help return your heart to a pure state.

Rather than chasing after the new, live a life in which you use the same objects for a long time. If you do this, you will naturally be able to care for and treasure the people around you as well.

When you repair a torn seam, you also begin to repair the relationship between yourself and others.

Even if you cannot completely restore an object back to its original state, you should **find a new way to use it**, and figure out how you can repurpose it within your daily life. A bucket that has developed a bad leak can still be useful as a pot for your garden. If you have a bamboo pole that you no longer use, with the addition of another one you can make a pair of stilts.

People who endlessly chase after new things have lost their freedom to earthly desire. Only those who can enjoy using their imaginations when working with limited resources know true freedom.

What sort of life do you wish to lead?

How to Repair

Containers and Tools

Pieces of pottery that have developed cracks can be beautifully restored at specialist shops using gold or silver. The screws of pans and kettles should occasionally be tightened, and these items should be sent for repairs if broken.

Clothes

Favourite garments always seem to get damaged the soonest. If you patch up holes, your clothes can become as good as new again. Socks that develop holes should also be darned.

Books

Pages that you frequently read often fall out first, but these can be re-glued and read again. For smaller tears, use tape, while a specialist can deal with damage that is difficult to repair on your own.

Deodorization

There are many people who tell me that the fragrance of the incense burned at temples relaxes them. Though the smell of incense always fills the halls of Buddhist temples, it is because the temple is a simple place that it helps to enhance the scent of the incense.

The basic principle behind deodorization is the exchange of old air for new. Always look for ways to improve the flow of air in your home, and **live at one with air.** Allow yourself to feel the present. If you put this idea into practice, not only will your heart feel refreshed and new, but you will also become less irritable.

How to Deodorize

Though the lovely smell of incense at the temple is supported by yin, or shadow, the materials that it is actually made out of are usually charcoal and green tea. The kinokuni *citrus tree and spike winter hazel are particularly popular for producing high-grade charcoal, which can be used not only for decorative purposes, but also for emergency heating.*

When choosing decorative pieces for the interior of your home, try pairing together seasonal flowers and fruit. Another popular deodorizer used at temples, which you can try when expecting guests, is placing the dried dregs of green tea or coffee in your entrance or toilet.

備長炭は
インテリアにも、
いざというときの
燃料にも
なります

Mould

Exactly why is it that mould grows?

Well, since mould is a living organism, when it finds a good place to live it settles there. Places that mould are particularly fond of include areas with little sunlight, little air, and lots of moisture.

No matter its purpose, a room with nothing in it is a place where mould will not grow. However, a room filled to the brim with so many things that they can no longer be organized, where sunlight is blocked, the airflow is restricted and moisture builds up, is the kind of environment that's perfect for mould. A room filled with so many things that they can no longer be organized is proof of a clouded heart. **The growth of mould in a room coincides with the growth of mould in the heart.**

The best way to prevent mould is to not keep things that are prone to become mouldy. The other way is to avoid creating environments in which mould can grow.

In order to do this **you must not hold on to unnecessary objects, and you must not put unnecessary things in**

a room. It is vital that you get rid of anything that you do not need.

Keep your home well organized, and make sure to completely dry an item before putting it away. Be particularly selective with the things you choose to leave around areas where there is water; the key is to remove all moisture. By being mindful not to create damp environments, you will also be mindful not to create spaces where mould can grow.

Moisture often appears on the panes of windows in modern, airtight buildings, leading to the growth of mould. If this happens in your home, be sure to completely wipe the windows down and remove all moisture. If you completely remove all the moisture from the windows, there is no need to use an antibacterial spray. This is all you need to do to prevent mould.

Rooms where mould grows are good for neither the body nor the heart.

Completely remove any dampness, and always keep your home clean.

5

Outside the Home

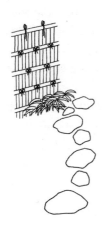

Windows

Glass is the very symbol of transparency and non-attachment. If your windows are cloudy or dusty, your mind will become cloudy as well.

Buddhist teachings stress the importance of shattering the blurry filter of the self, and viewing the world around you as it truly is. See and accept things the way they are. Learning to do so will help you achieve a state of enlightenment.

An ideal window will be cleaned to the point where you don't even notice that there is glass there, and you can enjoy the view without distraction. Try your hand at cleaning your windows until they are free of any spots of dirt or cloudiness.

How to Clean Your Windows

Newspaper will come in handy when cleaning glass. Lightly crumple a piece of newspaper, apply a small amount of soap and water, then wipe your windows until they are squeaky clean.

Newspaper is much better than rags or towels when cleaning windows. Unlike paper, towels tend to leave little hairs and other particulates on glass surfaces. Start by tackling the big smudges, then wipe systematically from one side to the other, going back and forth with the newspaper on a given spot before moving on. The job is done once there is no more moisture left.

You can use shop-bought soap, or use what is already in your cupboard. Soapy water with vinegar added to it is a great cleaning solution.

Screens

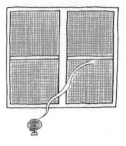

Be sure not to forget about your screens when you clean your windows. Remember that window screens are exposed to the outside, and are much dirtier than you may think. Since the outside air passes through your screens, dirty screens means dirty air. Clean them carefully, making sure that there is no grime in the countless tiny holes in the mesh.

A person cannot live if their breathing is compromised. Proper breathing is not only an integral part of Zen meditation, it is the flow that connects your body to the world around you.

Think of your windows as the way your house breathes. If your screens are gunked up, the air becomes stagnant, and your house starts to suffocate. Clean your screens well, and maintain a healthy flow of air between the inside and the outside.

How to Clean Your Screens

Wiping screens down regularly should be enough to keep them looking nice. However, very dirty screens should be removed from their frame, then taken outside and cleaned with a hose. Using a sponge or scouring pad is a great way to get into all the nooks and crannies.

Clean your screens as if you are cleaning your soul, allowing the air to flow through freely.

Once you have cleaned your screens, be sure to let them dry thoroughly before putting them back. If they are not completely dry, the excess moisture will drip into the window frame as well as on to the ground, attracting dust and dirt.

Gardens

Your garden is a place where you can get in touch with nature. Humans can't survive for long out in the wilderness, but we also can't survive without it. The garden is where we can observe and learn about the delicate balance that allows us, and indeed our plants, to exist.

Different temples have different types of gardens, each with its own individual character. What a person sees in a garden is a reflection of what is in their heart.

Because our gardens are a part of nature, they never look exactly the same twice. Start by listening to the voices of the vegetation around you. Notice how the voice within you responds. Your garden is a place where your body and soul can be in dialogue with your surroundings.

Gardening tools can rust easily, so you should treat them with care. As we have seen, if you don't keep your tools in proper working condition, they will become less and less effective, and the risk of injury will be increased. After every use you should clean the dirt off them, then give them a once-over with a grindstone. Be sure they are fully dry before putting them away. If you do this, your tools will always be in tip-top condition when you need them.

One important thing about gardening is to decide on a sensible amount that you would like to get done on the day. Don't push yourself too much. If you always leave a little bit of fuel in your tank, you will always be ready to return outside and get your hands dirty again. Go out there and engage with nature!

Gardening work is done mornings and evenings at temples. Get started in the morning, take a rest in the afternoon when the sun is at its hottest, then resume in the evening.

It is essential to stay hydrated while you work. We take tea breaks at ten in the morning and three in the afternoon. Taking regular breaks like this allows us to stay energized throughout the day.

We try to avoid using weedkiller. This is because it can be harmful to creatures such as earthworms and moles, and can negatively affect the quality of the soil. In order to have the best soil possible, you need to look out for nature as a whole. After all, all living things are connected.

Communing with nature gives richness to our minds. Examine nature, and then examine yourself through the lens of nature. You might be surprised at what you find.

Tending Your Garden

Monks find that cotton gloves and cotton socks are quite handy for gardening. They are comfortable and easy to clean if you get them dirty. We often wrap a towel or handkerchief around our head for protection from the sun as well.

If your garden is looking a bit dreary you should water it, weed it and then cut the grass. In order to get down to the roots, allow your sickle to just penetrate the soil's surface. Going too deep will cake your tools with dirt and you will end up making large holes in the ground.

Terraces

There is one corner of the grounds at my temple dubbed Kamiyacho Open Terrace that is open to the public. On weekdays many people working in the area bring their *bento* and perhaps a beverage here around lunchtime. It has come to be called *Otera* Café (Temple Café).

The terrace at the temple is similar to a terrace or decking area at your home. It is a place to sip drinks and entertain guests on sunny days, or spend time with your family at the weekend. In order to create a space where people can sit and relax, it is important to be attentive to clutter and grime. **Hospitality starts with cleanliness.** Be sure to make it a beautiful place where anyone can feel content.

Setting Up Your Terrace

Creating a space where you can relax and clear your mind requires adequate plant life. If your decking area or terrace faces out towards your garden, you should always keep that garden nicely kept. If it doesn't, you should get hold of subtle plants and greenery to bring a feeling of nature to your surroundings.

When expecting company, be sure to thoroughly wipe down your outdoor chairs, tables, handrails, and any other surfaces your guests might touch during their visit. Be sure to look high and low for things like spider webs as well.

Walkways

Temples will often have a long walkway, called a *sando*, leading up to the main building. The people who come to worship will take this path all the way to the altar, where they will straighten up their posture and offer a prayer. As we walk this path we prepare our hearts to come face to face with Buddha.

Although the average home does not have or need a *sando*, the path up to your door is the same idea. As you leave your home to face the day in the morning, and indeed as you come home in the evening, it represents the fantastic possibilities the day has to offer, and a safe place to rest once the day is done.

When you are on the path, try to stop at some point and take a deep breath, and let yourself be filled with gratitude.

Uchimizu

We have a practice called uchimizu *wherein we sprinkle water on to a street or path, cooling down the area as well as damping down dust and other particulates. Uchimizu was originally practised at Shinto shrines.*

If you know what time your family member or loved one is coming home, why not give uchimizu *a try? It is a way to express gratitude that the person has come home safely, and to instil happiness in them with the thought that someone has been awaiting their arrival.*

Even those of us living in a block of flats can do this. Think of the walk leading up to your front door as your sando. *Showing respect to all those who share this path is sure to send ripples of gratitude through your neighbourhood and your community.*

A Monk`s Guide to a Clean House and Mind

6

Body and Mind

Breathing

People who practise yoga are no doubt familiar with this, but there is a centuries-old Indian tradition of using proper breathing to calm the mind and body. It is said that even after achieving enlightenment Shakyamuni sat in quiet meditation beneath the Bodhi tree and continued to focus on correct breathing.

Breathing is what keeps us alive, whether we are sleeping or awake. Without us having to do anything our heart beats, our blood flows, our food is digested, and we breathe through our lungs. But among these involuntary bodily processes there is one that you can control: your breathing.

When you begin to lose your composure, your breathing will also become disturbed. This is proof that the two are connected. Be conscious of how you breathe, and make each breath count.

How to Breathe Properly

Exhaling and inhaling are the foundations of good breathing. Before breathing in, you should breathe out the contents of your lungs completely. Correcting your breathing will have a positive effect on your mind, allowing you to feel more balanced.

1   Take a long, slow exhaling breath through your mouth, focusing on the spot just below your belly button. Imagine that you are squeezing the air out of that spot.
2   Once you have exhaled fully, begin inhaling through your nose, again focusing on the spot below your belly button. This time, picture that you are filling that spot with air.

Washing Your Face

Cleaning doesn't only apply to your surroundings. I would also like to talk about how to clean your body and mind.

For example, **you should wash your face first thing in the morning.** Obviously face-washing is an everyday practice in every home, but did you know that it has a deeper meaning?

There is an old Zen teaching that says that if you haven't washed your face, everything you do throughout the day will be impolite and hasty. You don't wash your face because it is dirty. Washing your face is important regardless of how clean or dirty it might be.

You must not go out in public until you have washed your face.

Cleansing your skin and purifying your mind before you face the day is the bedrock of common courtesy.

At Eihei Temple we wash our faces with a *senmen-jukin*, an over two-metre-long towel used specifically for this purpose. We roll up our sleeves beforehand so as not to splash water on our robes.

We never use more than one bucketful of water. The water in the bucket is for washing our head and face, and brushing our teeth. Water is a blessing from nature, without which humans could not exist. We should use that blessing well, never wasting a drop. We should wash our faces with a sense of gratitude to nature.

I understand that most people are not going to wash their faces like this at home and that most people don't own the items that I have described. But we can still commit ourselves to conserving water and not leaving the tap running while we are out of the room. Rinse your towel well once you have finished, then hang it out to dry.

Don't underestimate the good that can come from washing your face. The fact that it is a part of your daily routine is all the more reason why you should be mindful and deliberate while you do it.

This is the key to a sound mind.

How to Wash Your Face

Fill a small bucket or other container with water. The main goal here is not removing dirt, and soap is not needed. Start with your forehead, then go on to the eyebrows, eyes, nose, and so on, moving downwards. Then clean from behind your ears to the tip of your chin.

Clean your face and your mind will become clearer. No matter how early you get up, you will be able to feel refreshed. Your heart and soul will be revitalized before you know it.

Brushing Your Teeth

Our mouths are one of the most important parts of our body.

Eating, speaking and breathing all involve the mouth. Buddhist teachings talk of *shinkui no sango*, which refers to the three types of behaviours that humans engage in, involving the mind, body and mouth. They teach that we must polish our behaviours associated not just with mind and body, but also with our mouth. Brushing your teeth is a way to keep your main channel for communicating with others clean. Be sure to be thorough and attentive when you do this.

How to Brush Your Teeth

In a Zen temple brushing your teeth is something that we pay great attention to. The Zen master Dogen taught that you should brush your teeth as if you were putting a fine polish on them.

To prevent cavities, it is of course important to thoroughly clean in the spaces between your teeth. Master Dogen stressed the importance of doing this as well as brushing your tongue.

Cleanliness is close to enlightenment, and so is a clean mouth with a fresh breath.

A Monk`s Guide to a Clean House and Mind

Meals

すべて入れ子状にしまえるスグレモノ

応量器

In this busy modern age, far too many of us rush our meals, barely even noticing what exactly we are consuming. This is a great shame.

We all know that humans cannot live without food. Your body is made of the food you eat, and therefore neglecting to consider how and what you eat is the same as neglecting your body. By neglecting your body you are neglecting your mind.

Food is what creates and sustains us, so let's all pay a little bit more attention to what we eat.

People who are interested in Japanese tea probably know that it was originally brought to Japan as a medicine. You really cannot discuss the traditional Japanese tea ceremony without any mention of Buddhism. We think of our manners during meal time as just as important as during a formal tea ceremony.

During my time at Hongan Temple in Kyoto, everyone would put their hands together in prayer before meals, give words of thanks in chorus, then proceed to eat in silent gratitude. You too should try eating a meal deliberately, enjoying each individual bite to the fullest.

Know just how much food is enough. Aim to stop when you are about 80 per cent full. If you make sure to truly enjoy each bite of food, you may find that you feel full and satisfied much sooner. Learn to do this and you will never overeat again.

Shinshin ichinyo refers to the idea that the mind and the body are one. Trying to think of them as separate is folly. Meals, manners and gratitude: put these elements together and you too can live in harmony.

Meal Etiquette

Even at home you can show your gratitude before and after meals by putting your hands together and reciting a Buddhist prayer. Here are two of the traditional prayers.

Shokuzen – before meals: 'Many lives, and much hard work, have gone into the blessing that is this meal. I will show my appreciation by enjoying this food with a deep sense of gratitude.'

Shokugo – after meals: 'I thank you for the wonderful meal, with deep gratitude, respect and reverence.'

Haircuts

Many people probably associate monks with shaved heads. Indeed, monks of most sects sport this look. In some of the sects that do not require this practice, the head is still shaved when one first becomes a monk. This shows that you are committed to entering the priesthood and letting worldly things go.

I'm guessing most readers probably get their hair cut when it starts to get a little bit long or shaggy. Monks at the Eihei Temple shave their heads on days that end in '4' or '9'. Why not give this approach a try? Even if you are not shaving your head, cutting your hair at regular intervals is a way to hone your self-discipline.

How to Shave

Monks at Eihei Temple do not use soap or shaving cream when they shave their heads and faces.

Many an inexperienced monk has drawn blood when first learning to shave in a temple. An absolute minimum of water is needed with little or no additions. Because only plain water is used, it can be returned safely to nature once you have finished your shave.

Bodily Functions

This might sound strange, but every time I visit the toilet I am struck with how amazing the human body is. We eat food, and our bodies digest that food and absorb the nutrients. Our bodies then get rid of whatever is left over. Sweat and earwax are the same idea. The human body automatically cleanses itself regularly. It works tireless 24 hours a day, 365 days a year. We should all feel grateful for this.

We initially learn from our parents how to use the toilet as children, but after that we are on our own. We never see what other people do in the toilet, and so I am guessing that we all have our own way of going about the task, never giving it much thought.

But using the toilet in a Zen temple is done carefully and deliberately. As we have seen, in Zen Buddhism the toilet is considered a sacred place. This is why we carry out our bodily functions in such a prescribed way.

Before using the toilet, we set our bucket of water in a specific spot. We face the toilet with our left hand on our

A Monk`s Guide to a Clean House and Mind

hip, position our right hand in a position called *tanji*. Picture your index finger plucking your thumb like a guitar string. That is *tanji*. We do this three times before and after we finish using the toilet.

The proper way to clean our private areas once we finish is not with toilet paper but with the water from our bucket. We use our left hand to clean ourselves, just like the traditional method in India.

A bathroom stall is a place where a monk gets a short rest, away from the rest of his peers. But it is possible to get lazy if one indulges in this privacy too much. It is especially important to stay alert and present, remembering one's devotion to staying pure.

You can create a clean and comfortable place for you and your loved ones to take care of business. Every time you step into your toilet you should appreciate how your body is expelling toxins and waste. You should feel refreshed and grateful.

Toilet Etiquette

Using the toilet is one of the most basic, primal behaviours that we engage in. Let's do it mindfully every time. Always keep the toilet slippers straight, and the paper looking nice and fresh. Just like the rest of the home, the toilet is a place to be considerate of others as well as yourself.

Sleep

In a temple we always go to bed early, and rise early. As long as you don't stay up too late, you will be able to remain active throughout the day regardless of how early you may have woken up.

We work hard all day, then read aloud from sacred texts, effectively using up all of our energy. When it is time to crawl into bed, our bodies never protest. We don't have trouble falling asleep, and we always naturally get the right amount of sleep.

The word 'Buddha' literally means 'awakened one'.

Tips for a Good Sleep
Make it a point to keep regular hours, and make the most of your time while the sun is out.

Be sure to get up and move around throughout the day, and go to bed early. Sleeping longer than what your body actually requires is nothing short of lazy. Succumbing to sleep gluttony is giving in to your worldly desires. Idly sleeping your days away is no way to live.

A Monk`s Guide to a Clean House and Mind

When the Cleaning
is Finished

You might be surprised to see the tiny spaces where monks live during their training. Zen monks are each allotted a single square of *tatami* mat (180 cm by 85 cm), where they are to eat, meditate and sleep.

Even in the *Jodoshinshu* branch of Buddhism, monks live together in close quarters. Writing utensils and undergarments beyond the bare minimum are forbidden. About ten people live, work, clean and study together day in and day out, all in complete silence. There is simply no room for idle, worldly thoughts.

Quite honestly a life free of possessions is very comfortable. After Ippen Shonin's pilgrimage, he continued living a life without possessions, and never again settled down to live in one specific place. **By not being anchored down by worldly possessions, his mind was able to achieve true freedom.**

There are some things you start to realize when living the Zen life of simplicity. Namely, that you only keep things of good quality. They are the final products of many people's diligent work. They are the kinds of things that you can continue to use again and again for many years.

When you acquire such items you begin to truly understand why they must be treasured. This is because the blood, sweat and tears of the person or people who created them have become part of them. Conversely, if you are surrounded only by poor-quality objects that you don't care about, it is impossible to understand what it is to truly value something.

Even if there are young children in your home, you should try and limit possessions to only high-quality products. For example, teach your children from a young age how to treat fine dishware and utensils properly. Children who grow up like this will gain an appreciation of what makes an item valuable.

Scrutinize merchandise thoroughly when you shop, and consider whether or not you truly need an item before purchasing it. Also consider whether or not you can live comfortably with it. Having fewer possessions in your home will make cleaning it much easier, and, as we have seen, although handcrafted items cost a little bit more, they will stand the test of time

There is an old Zen saying that goes, 'Where there is nothing, there is everything.' By letting go of everything, you can open up a universe of unlimited possibilities.

Organization

Monks live in very simple surroundings indeed. They only have the bare minimum of possessions, and those possessions are all stored away in predetermined areas. This means that even their very small living spaces are never cluttered.

Every item is stored in its proper place. It might sound obvious, but in how many homes can you actually see this? Take out an item when you need it, then return it immediately upon finishing your task. It is very easy, so why do so many of us struggle to do it? Because we have become reckless about how we deal with our possessions. That is to say, our minds have become reckless.

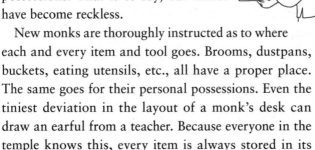

New monks are thoroughly instructed as to where each and every item and tool goes. Brooms, dustpans, buckets, eating utensils, etc., all have a proper place. The same goes for their personal possessions. Even the tiniest deviation in the layout of a monk's desk can draw an earful from a teacher. Because everyone in the temple knows this, every item is always stored in its proper place.

A monk friend of mine told me something funny: 'In the beginning I was simply putting things in their proper spots because I had been told to do so. But through repetition I actually began to hear the items speak to me. I felt like if I listened closely enough, I would naturally know where the object needed to go.'

'I see,' is all the response I could offer.

Listen to the voice of the object. This is a tall order if you allow your mind to become restless.

Use your possessions carefully, and listen closely with your heart. Sooner or later you will begin to hear the voice as well. As you do so, you should also try to be knowledgeable about where to store things in your living space. Think of your home as an allegory for your body.

Keep cleaning it every day. **An object will tell you where it wants to be kept if you learn to see its true essence.** All of us can achieve that state of mind!

Experiencing the Seasons

Life in a temple reflects the changing seasons.

From New Year's Day until the cherry blossoms of spring, and from the Lantern Festival in summer until the turning of the leaves in autumn, monks living in a temple have no lack of opportunities to celebrate the gentle transition from one season into the next. This was one of the things that made me glad I became a monk.

They say that there is no place like Japan when it comes to appreciating all that the four seasons have to offer. Even in my temple in the middle of Tokyo we can enjoy the beautiful cherry and plum tree blossoms in the spring, the din of the cicadas in the summer, and the soft song of crickets in the autumn. Truly enjoying the seasons is most important to Japanese people.

Clean your home thoroughly and then let the seasons pour in. There are many ways to enjoy the seasons in traditional Japanese rooms. Seasonal flowers adorn the *tokonoma*, and the decorative hanging scroll is replaced by one that reflects the season as well. Burning incense that evokes the season is good too. The traditional *shoji* doors keep the heat in during the winter, while *yoshido*, their thinner and more breathable counterparts, keep the room cool in summer. Even changing the paper on the *shoji* becomes more enjoyable when you are working in step with the seasons.

We change our outfits in the spring and autumn. The robes we wear have summer and winter versions. On the first day of wearing our summer clothing, the cool breeze blows up our sleeves and through the thinner fabric. On the other hand, the weight of the thicker winter clothes portends the coming of winter. Some of our work clothing has a thick lining, while some does not.

This doesn't mean of course that we have a wardrobe full of different outfits. We have three basic ones based on what we are doing that day. By living with such a limited amount of clothing options, we are free from ever having to worry about what to wear. By stripping away unnecessary possessions, and living simply, we can enjoy the seasons and our surroundings to the fullest extent.

Get up and open a window. Take in the fresh air that blows through. The smell of the wind changes from season to season. The sounds of insects and the songs of birds tell us what season it is. Day in, day out, time marches forward and the seasons slowly shift. Buddha comes through nature and reaches out to us all. The nature you see around you is reflecting back at you what is in your heart.

Spring Cleaning

Everything is made spick and span on a daily basis in a temple, so there is no need for spring cleaning, right? **Wrong.** Of course we clean the floors, kitchen, toilet and bathroom every day. The places that are hard to reach are cleaned regularly as well. This means that nothing in the temple is cleaned only once a year. In terms of cleaning dirt from surfaces, spring cleaning is not necessary in a temple.

However, as we have seen, cleaning is meant to clean dirt from your heart and your soul. Spring cleaning is a way to clear your mind of all the grime that has accumulated over the course of the year. So, as you can see, this annual cleaning is quite important in a temple.

The common Japanese practice of doing a thorough cleaning at the end of the year was once referred to as *susuharai*, which literally described the cleaning of soot. Back in the time of wood stoves, candles and oil lamps, soot would begin to accumulate here and there throughout the living space. The practice of doing a thorough cleaning is still called *susuharai* in some temples even to this day.

In mid-December, the Honganji Temple puts on a *susuharai* event where the general public can participate in cleaning the temple alongside monks. After the monks finish their early morning chores, the monks, the visitors and the head priest all meet and pray together. They then sweep the altar of the Buddha statue with a giant broom about 4 m in length. The same ritual is performed in front of the statue of Shinran. After this everyone lines up side by side and the cleaning begins.

Keeping with the old tradition, we beat the *tatami* mats with a long bamboo pole. We then use a big fan to blow the dust away, finally using a broom to clean up the rest. Perhaps what we call spring cleaning is less about the cleaning and more of an event. We are all celebrating having made it through another year with one another. There is no greater gift than that.

The bonds you have with your friends and family are the foundation of a healthy mind. I highly recommend spring cleaning as an annual event in your family. It is important to focus on the places in your home that you rarely get around to cleaning. As for dividing up cleaning tasks between family members, bear in mind that it is good for everyone to get the opportunity to clean areas of the home that they are not accustomed to cleaning. Doing the spring cleaning together will strengthen and deepen the bonds between you.